BY THE RIVER MANDOVI

ELIZABETH DENNINGS

Copyright © Elizabeth Dennings
All Rights Reserved.

This book has been self-published with all reasonable efforts taken to make the material error-free by the author. No part of this book shall be used, reproduced in any manner whatsoever without written permission from the author, except in the case of brief quotations embodied in critical articles and reviews.

The Author of this book is solely responsible and liable for its content including but not limited to the views, representations, descriptions, statements, information, opinions and references ["Content"]. The Content of this book shall not constitute or be construed or deemed to reflect the opinion or expression of the Publisher or Editor. Neither the Publisher nor Editor endorse or approve the Content of this book or guarantee the reliability, accuracy or completeness of the Content published herein and do not make any representations or warranties of any kind, express or implied, including but not limited to the implied warranties of merchantability, fitness for a particular purpose. The Publisher and Editor shall not be liable whatsoever for any errors, omissions, whether such errors or omissions result from negligence, accident, or any other cause or claims for loss or damages of any kind, including without limitation, indirect or consequential loss or damage arising out of use, inability to use, or about the reliability, accuracy or sufficiency of the information contained in this book.

Made with ♥ on the Notion Press Platform
www.notionpress.com

To Eliora
my niece

Contents

Copyright	*vii*
Preface	*ix*
Acknowledgements	*xix*
1. Rational Thought	1
2. Society And Politics	13
3. Queer Conundrums	25
4. Prejudice	40
5. Love Of A Numdilect	50
6. Self-Care	65
7. Life Lessons	74
8. Ecology	82
Notes to the Poems	85

Copyright

Copyright © 2024 by Elroy Anthony Savio Rebello

All rights reserved.

No part of this publication may be reproduced, distributed, or transmitted in any form or by any means, including photocopying, recording, or other electronic or mechanical methods, without the prior written permission of the publisher, except as permitted by Indian copyright law. For permission requests, contact the author at denningselizabeth@gmail.com

Preface

Poetry has never brought me in enough money to buy shoestrings.
- William Wordsworth

Why do we write poetry? I have believed most earnestly, that there must always be a good reason for a civilized human to engage in any activity. In the 21st century, everything must amount to something substantive. We educate ourselves to secure employment and to sustain employment, we engage in additional training through workshops and short term courses; employment is necessary to earn a decent livelihood. So, how does poetry fit into this scheme? Is it a crucial skill for employment?

We may engage in poetry simply to be creative, to express ourselves tersely, but we certainly do not use it as the main source of communication. Perhaps we use it to explore various human emotions like love, pain, and solitude. It may also help us understand history, politics, and society. It may even provide us with a fresh perspective to life. I guess, poetry is one of those human urges akin to love. I never intended to love him with such unflinching truth when I first saw him, unable to even get his name right. I was never an ardent student-fan of poetry. It just happened, unintentionally. Poetry is an organic urge to translate a mental and musical play into human language.

PREFACE

The main purpose of poetry is to illuminate realities which are at times undecipherable and trapped in history, politics, and society--most often understood at a superficial level. It is an instrument to unravel the truth. Certainly, we can write on love, happiness, and all that is joyous but reality cannot be accepted in isolation of all that is bitter or sorrowful. One would be foolish to only expect happiness in their life and to cave in like a braying donkey when struck with sorrow. A poet must not shy away from their responsibility to depict the truth and must undertake the creation of verses as an independent judge passing the fairest judgment. As the dialogue goes in the Bollywood movie, *Party* (1984) "Koi bhi political system ho, anyay aur daman ke virudh awaz uthana kalakar ki ahem zimmedari hai."

By the River Mandovi is my second experiment with self-publishing a book of poems. I hope you enjoyed some verses from my first book, *Rhetorics of a Misfit* (2023). That book was more of an infant's first step which introduced me to the nuances of self-publishing that has made me a better poet and publisher. I hope you will be intrigued by this current collection of poems.

My poems do not adhere to conventions of any particular age and are largely in free verse, however, there are some which are accompanied with a decent metre and rhyme scheme. As a poet, I stand quite comfortably between traditional and Instagram poets for I am neither too sophisticated nor too dull! I cannot certainly be an Insta(gram) poet, because the social media app seems to gobble up a considerable portion of precious time which can be applied towards productive endeavours. There is, in my experience, something malevolent about Instagram that slays discipline and stunts intellectual growth. How can one benefit from endless scrolling on the app? Additionally, I cannot be an Insta poet because my poetry is not instant noodles! Conceiving and reading poetry requires time for it to be fully grasped just like a bud that blossoms into a marvellous flower. Doesn't that require time? The nature of Instagram doesn't allow for such time and space for it inundates us with instant information, like a mukbang for the mind!

Poetry at least requires three readings: for the literary devices, for personal meaning, and for the contextual interpretation. Reading verses is like taking in the beauty of nature or the love of our life, one glance is never enough, like our most cherished song played in a loop for hours together. As William Wordsworth noted, ". . .verse will be red a hundred times where the prose is read once...."

We are eternally encapsulated by language, and most of us wish to master the English language. In the pursuit of this goal we undertake majors and/or postgraduate courses in English, but the completion of these courses *per se* does not guarantee a mastery of the language. I know with certainty that some individuals complete the M.A in English without ever reading any of the required texts. There is more politics in the Departments of English than English itself! One of my departmental heads, to quench her grudge against me, waged a squabble against my emphasis on literary devices. Literary devices are to literature what salt is to food, sugar is to cake, fragrance is to a rose, and the soul is to the body!

PREFACE

In my humble opinion, a student who desires to major or pursue an M.A in English must focus on being a good writer or teacher or both. They must also shed the guilt that reading literature is not as serious a task as studying economics, psychology, law, etc. Choosing the study of literary texts is the most natural form of education one can undertake. How often do we recall what we've rote-learned? But that which we've loved is comparatively durable. It resides in the mind as an indelible impression. Consider Ruskin Bond's description of the flowing mountain spring in *Rain in the Mountains*: "The water of the mountain stream, always in a hurry, bubbling over rocks and chattering, 'I'm late, I'm late!…'" or the reportage of a most passionate emotion by Pablo Neruda in *100 Love Sonnets*: "I love you as certain dark things are to be loved, in secret, between the shadow and the soul." So, jettison this guilt and sit by your study table or on your bed, carefree, and read! That is the pivotal step to effective writing and by extension, effective speaking.

Reading is not sufficient. It is essential that one must read good books: the classics, the indisputables, and those written by awardees of the Booker Prize. I have also been recently aware, in addition to English teachers who do not read literature, of poets who do not read poems! The following reading list can do much good to an aspiring poet:

i. *The Oxford Book of English Verses* edited by Christopher Ricks
ii. *The Complete Works of Shakespeare* edited by Peter Alexander
iii. The various dramas by Christopher Marlowe and William Shakespeare by Roma Gill
iv. *The Holy Bible* (King James Version)

v. Works by your favourite poet.

With these as your basic companions, your growth cannot be impeded by the so called writer's block. I certainly believe it to be an excuse of the lazy writer and we all have at some point been guilty of it. The very act of writing poetry is an orchestral performance alongside your Muse, the poets gone by, and classical music. As I write this preface I'm listening to Luke Faulkner's *Daydreaming*. Some of my preferred contemporary composers to listen to while I write include Ludovico Einaudi, Denis Stelmakh, Jordan Critz, and Virginio Aiello. Music seems to do away with the dams that obstruct the natural flow of the mighty river!

You might be curious about my pen name. The choice wasn't solely mine; I would've been perfectly content using my given name, Elroy A. S. Rebello. Similarly, the decision to deviate from the gender was also not entirely mine; I could've easily chosen a pen name that suits a cisgender man. But who determines what name is appropriate for men and women? A man and woman, can both be named Krishna, Aisha, Iqbal, Zaynab, Andrew or Mary and the world will still stay intact. The French philosopher Simone de Beauvoir posited, "One is not born, but rather becomes, a woman." While for some, womanhood, may have been bestowed upon them by birth, it was shoved upon me by society in the most brutish way possible as I was an effeminate boy. I have been conscious of my femininity just as life within my being but social construct did not allow for it. So as I navigated life in my natural and fabulous femininity as a naive boy in the way I spoke, walked, and lived, I was made aware of the woman in me through degrading foul language that parents pass on to their children. This language is used as an assertion of contempt towards effeminate men in Goa, words like: bile, bizuaon huicho, baizon, hijra, chakka, ladies, and fifty-fifty. As I recall these troubled childhood episodes, I am overwhelmed by an inexplicable sorrow but that is what any artist must do to produce art: study the anatomy of their pain. In this manner, society instilled a shame in me for the woman within, this is how I was made aware of her presence. She has suffered at the hands of society and propelled by society, sometimes, I've shunned her as a witch. Scarred by society, I'm not even half the woman I was supposed to be, while I do see on social media a handful of men who were able to sustain their inner woman and let her flourish. My message to any teenage queer boy or girl is to nourish and treasure their femininity or masculinity in defiance of society for it isn't worth conforming to social norms on gender. Therefore, my pen name is a response to transform the shame imposed by society into freedom, dignity, and resilience. The name Elizabeth is derived from one of the most powerful monarch of England and Ireland, Queen Elizabeth I, while the last name, Dennings, is drawn from Lord Alfred Tom Denning, the most influential judge of the 20th century. Both these figures were introduced to me in my college years as I explored a bit of history and a lot of the laws.

This book is divided into various categories: rational thought, society and politics, queer conundrums, prejudice, love of a numdilect (a person who has never been loved), selfcare, life, and ecology. One might wonder why I write about love. What can the numdilect offer on the subject? I write about love for the same reason as a priest offers marriage advice! I hope you like some of my poetry, which largely serve as social criticism. I unabashedly admit that I write poems to bring my readers a tad closer to the truth. Here, it is pertinent to briefly discuss some of the poems that this book has to offer.

By the River Mandovi We Sat down and Wept features in the first category, 'Rational Thought,' and is written in five sections which depicts a clash of contrary beliefs between lovers as they navigate their respective convictions in faith and reason. Here is an excerpt from the poem:

> ...The scriptures are the greatest instruments of truth,
> Guiding men through the vices of tempestuous youth,
> Providing us answers when science has none,
> Passed on by ancestors making us with God, one...
> ...Who says religion is the filler to all unanswered question?
> Is not our independent opinion a result of indoctrination?
> Is not our view fed to us by the church, government, and family?
> Are we truly in cognizance of our most pure reality?...
> ...Do you see what I see, my dearest and pure one?
> Can two diverse minds, on pivotal matters, agree?...

The second category, 'Society and Politics,' offers poetic critique on certain issues that torment the heart as we witness the ghoulish reality. *Poubius and Mithunaur* is a tale of Manipur drawn from its history, mythology, and current state of affairs. *Siro Devi* portrays the life of a midwife from Bihar and her damning confession. Consider this snippet from the poem:

PREFACE

I am a Dai,

The one who

Brings solace to

Women in labour,

Who guides life into

This world; oh, what joy!

Tis only a woman who can give life,

Tis only a woman who can take it away...

The third category, 'Queer Conundrums,' represents the life of an individual from the LGBTQIA+ community as they experience love, freedom, and shame. *Grotesque* portrays the journey of a queer person from childhood to adulthood. Here is a glimpse of it:

...As a child:

Come dance with me on my footstool

To the F.M music playing on the radio,

The Bollywood hits,

Come feel the girl in me,

Come feel the insolence,

When I was always being me,

Come feel the touch of my landlord,

Come feel the disappointment of my folks,

Come dance with me on my footstool...

Are You a Boy or a Girl? is a reproduction of a surreal experience which questions the heteronormative gender binary in a subtle manner. The poem, I humbly believe, is filled with vivid and delightful imagery:

PREFACE

> . . .The bus halts with a jerk: ho-ham,
> To take on board a woman:
> Dusky and dirty,
> Clad in a ghagra choli,
> Covered with mirrors
> That reflect our fears,
> And her sunny ghunghat hanging by the bun. . .

The section, 'Prejudice,' can guide the reader into a deeper understanding of human biases which are at times unconscious and sometimes, to our horror, conscious. We don't need to look into history to understand this state of mind. The greatest example of it is the prejudice of the Israeli government against the Palestinians. *Prism* is a poem which questions such a conscious prejudice:

> . . . They are not human for you,
> You flinch to say with crisp clarity,
> Fearing judgment of the world,
> But you utter the unutterable,
> Trying to wield your ugly truth
> After gulping down a block of air,
> That slashes down your malice ridden throat;
> Is that your troth?
> Failure to conceive liberty,
> Failure to conceive a question,
> Failure to be real, raw, and civil. . .

Although the poems have been placed in one category, some of them may have an overlapping of more than one theme. The classification is based on the prominence of a theme in a poem and is intended for the convenience of my readers.

If you've made it this far in reading my preface, I am deeply humbled. I request that you leave a genuine review on Goodreads for this book; if you've purchased the book online, kindly post your review on the relevant online platform. As a self-publishing author with modest resources, your feedback shall help my book reach potential readers. I would also like to know your thoughts on my poems. Indubitably, readers are independent judges for authors, but social media has caused most of them to abdicate their judgeship.

Acknowledgements

Della Diniz and Cassie Mascarenhas for their advice and support.

Meta AI Business Assistant and Canva for providing the tools to design the perfect cover.

Notion Press for their publishing support.

1. Rational Thought

I. *<u>By the River Mandovi We Sat Down and Wept</u>*
A. *<u>The Communion</u>*
David:-

On the window sill Zaid sits, draped in moonlight,
Looking across the promenade by the Mandovi.
I stand confounded by a glorious sight:
His terrifying deep gaze, his tender cheeks, like a babe so holy.

I surrender to the infinite abyss,
With a tremor and a caress to his sublime,
Unceasing, unshackled, over and over again, we kiss
So desperately as though running out of time.

Zaid:-

I wish not for my man's love to suspend,
Oh David, my desires are foolish and irrational.
How can one simply the Sun's movement amend,
To encase our passion into an unbreachable crystal?

David:-

My most sweetest boy, we shall in this moment be,
Without qualms and questions filled with divine glee.

B. <u>David's Arguments</u>
On the promenade by the Mandovi
We stand, our countenance fraught with a qualm,
Can two diverse minds, on pivotal matters, agree?
Can there be any point of relief, a soothing balm?

There was once a need for it all, religions
With all its gods, angels, and demons,
When reality was, due to human foibles, undecipherable,
When all, living and non-living, had a soul, our minds - gullible.

Pigs and boars we worshiped, plenty
With sacrifices: animals, women, and children,
For the Earth was our goddess, fierce yet motherly
And the Sun, our god, to ensure that she be with life laden.

The priests vouch for this world to be a few thousand years old,
That God exists as the scriptures provide, through epochs retold;
Can these retellings be true as the lustre of the celestial being above?
Or are they mere scrawls and squiggles of uncultured tribal cults of Jove?
It is the fossil which stares into our folly that is religion,
How could then we be created through hocus - pocus?
We've traversed through three hundred thousand years of evolution,

ELIZABETH DENNINGS

But to the wayside we throw logic and enthrall in life's circus.
Do you see what I see, my dearest and pure one?
Can two diverse minds, on pivotal matters, agree?

C. <u>Zaid's Rebuttal</u>

On the promenade by the Mandovi we stand,
With God in our hearts no evil can draw us away,
For there are questions which unravel only in his hand,
Who created us in his own image like a potter does with clay.

The scriptures are the greatest instruments of truth,
Guiding men through the vices of tempestuous youth,
Providing us answers when science has none,
Passed on by ancestors making us with God, one.

The peace of our realm is intrinsic with religions,
Enlightening us with worldly prophecies,
That scientists now claim as their own revelations,
Do you, my love, accede to what the believer sees?

For the Big Bang you shall find in 21:30 of Al-Anbiya'
When heaven and earth were brought apart, not a recent idea.
55:19 of Ar-Rahman reveals to us the salt wedge of two seas,
Do you, my love, accede to what the believer sees?
Look to the Bible if not my gleaming beacon,
God's sacrifice of his only Son, John 3:16 evinces,
He is the almighty who conjured up the Garden of Eden,
Do you, my love, accede to what the believer sees?
Look to the many Hindu texts if not my luminous guide,
Love, compassion, equanimity are virtues most glorified
In the Bhagavadgita 12:13-14 you may tolerantly delve,

Do you, my love, accede to what the believer sees?

Do you see what I see, my dearest and pure one?
Can two diverse minds, on pivotal matters, agree?

D. <u>David's Surrebuttal</u>

On the promenade by the Mandovi we sit,
As our hearts pump blood that sustain us whole,
As pillows of darkness engulf the sky that is moonlit,
We exist with bone and flesh, not a fictional soul.

Who says religion is the filler to all unanswered question?
Is not our independent opinion a result of indoctrination?
Is not our view fed to us by the church, government, and family?
Are we truly in cognizance of our most pure reality?

We grapple with evil which with brutish force afflicts
The innocent one who desperately flees.
Are not the scriptures the root of all human conflicts?
Do you, my most precious, accede to what the reasoner sees?

Science and religion were born in two minds markedly diverse,
One in the dark, the other in the light, both in converse,
You cite the scriptures as per your whims and fancies,
For Mandovi has a wedge and nature performs with a bang its many Tandav dances.

Look to the Bible if not my gleaming beacon,
Happiness for massacring infants, Psalms 137:9 evinces.
Is this love or gore of the heathen?
Do you, my most precious, accede to what the reasoner sees?

If the sciences are so intimately married to the religions,
Why the persecution of the queer who've been cleared of all perversions?
Leviticus 20:13 mandates death as if they be a contagious disease,
Do you, my most precious, accede to what the reasoner sees?

Look to the Quran if not my gleaming beacon,
The hate towards others in At-Tawbah 9:5 is seen with ease.
It is this vitriol which will our character weaken,
Do you, my most precious, accede to what the reasoner sees?

Look to the many Hindu texts if not my luminous guide,
The Bhagavadgita embodies not peace but fratricide,
And the Manusmriti divides humanity into castes,
Do you, my most precious, accede to what the reasoner sees?

Do you see what I see, my dearest and pure one?
Can two diverse minds, on pivotal matters, agree?

E. <u>The Parting</u>

David:-

By the river Mandovi we sat down and wept,
As the darkness ceased upon this twisted world,
And the grey sky, the ominous clouds, and the puddle-pelting rain
Acquiesced and a thunderous performance like an orchestra unfurled.

This species has been diverted from its natural terrain;
We feign joy, normality, calm, love, care, victimization,
Like air-rain strikes which disguise tears and pain,
Oh, what the homosapien's world could've been sans religion!

Zaid:-

As there seems to be no point where we can meet,
Let us part and bring an end to this tedious tussle,
I shall take my unflinching faith that is for me so sweet,
And you take your reason which does in evidence nestle.

David:-

I depart with a hope that you shall one day awaken,
That like Zeus and his entourage, religion shall lay forsaken!

II. *Azan*

How can music be evil
As some religions adjudge?
For it has appeared in the climax;
Crucial junctures in my life,
Shoving me into a catharsis,
Unshackling me from the anchors
Which held me down,
In the colossal and fear-inspiring
Depths of darkness!

Doesn't the Azan induce calm with its rhythm?
Don't we yearn for its melody everyday?

III. <u>Feelings</u>

I don't believe in supernatural things,
But the most pure are feelings:
Anger, sorrow, love, empathy,
And all others which one can be.

So when they express love,
See with kinder eyes!
Rather than give them a shove,
For this feeling is devoid of any lies.

So when they love with a dare,
Dismiss with human care,
Rather than jettison the dead body
Tied to a boulder in the sea.

I don't believe in supernatural things,
But the most pure are feelings:
Anger, sorrow, love, empathy,
And all others which one can be.

So when they surrender to you,
And admit sorrow which was due,
Reserve criticism for another day,
To be debated later when the hair turns grey.

So when they act with rage,

ELIZABETH DENNINGS

Be not foolish to react with hate,
Rather decipher the cause which is their cage,
And respond with empathy before its too late.

I don't believe in supernatural things,
But the most pure are feelings.

IV. Reading Poetry

Poetry is not to be read in a hurry,
For it is not a novel, drama or short story,
It is to be read first in its bare constitution,
It is to be read second in association
With knowledge of history,
Politics, society and self,
An interpretation neither foolhardy,
Nor too meek and feeble.

It is an art of a calm mind,
It is a skill of the brave,
For it takes you to the glories
Of birth and life,
For it takes you to the repulsions
Of death and decay.

It is an art of the truth seeker,
It is a skill of a just mind,
For one may be tempted to distort
The past, present, and the future.

Poetry is not to be read in a hurry,
For it is not a novel, drama or short story.

2. Society and Politics

I. <u>Siro Devi</u>

I am a Dai,
The one who
Brings solace to
Women in labour,
Who guides life into
This world; oh, what joy!
Tis only a woman who can give life,
Tis only a woman who can take it away.

I am a Dai,
I bring death to a newborn,
Compelled either by customs
Or by greed for Rs. 100, both firmly
Tied to the burden of a married woman;
When did I, a fragrant life giving blossom
Turn putrid to resonate repulsion and rot?
Tis only a woman who can give life,
Tis only a woman who can take it away.

I am a Dai,
Not educated in a school of medicine,

Knowing much more than the ones with a degree,
Much sort after to carry the cross of my foul society
Which turned me from a life-giver to an executioner,
Our axe: three spoons of salt down the infant's throat,
Our axe: three spoons of urea down the infant's throat,
Our axe: three maneuvers to twist the infant's neck!
Tis only a woman who can give life,
Tis only a woman who can take it away.

I am a Dai,
Today, I run from the ghosts
Who've haunted me for several decades
And choose not to cease.
I admit, I am in denial of my guilt,
But it is this denial that supplies life to my soul
Until I face the souls of the several who lay beneath
The earth on which I reside.
Tis only a woman who can give life,
There is none who can take it away!

II. <u>Poubius and Mithunaur</u>

Once upon a time there lived Poubius,
A dragon with a character of calm and ferocity,
With scales of amber and scarlet phosphorescence,
With the girth and length of General Sherman,
In an enchanted lake rich with Pengba.

Many equal beasts of fur and tusks and talons
Envied to conquer the enchanted lake,
For the soft Pengba with its nourishing oils,
But seldom were they a match to the mighty Poubius,
As they delivered a swift and mortal gash to its foes.

But deep in the dark psithurious forest of those who slither,
Lay the malevolent and vitriolic serpent god, Nagon;
Half man, half snake, a humanoid from head to torso
With several serpentine heads and tails
Jutting out from their trapezius and trunk.

Upon the hour of the darkest night
When Luna was courted by Jupiter,
And the weak hurried their little ones to sleep
Nagon struck with its most fatal bite
So as to breech the glow of amber on Poubius by the neck.

Clop. . .clop. . .clop. . .clop. . .clop. . .clop
Came the clatter of hooves that moved the crust,

Two glows moved towards Nagon as they moved
To deliver the venomous blight on Poubius,
And with a thud and thump Nagon was flung
In the garden where Jupiter was engaged intensely with Luna.

As Helios reached the scene of the battle there stood
Mithunaur, the ripped ox with their menacing horns and hooves,
Tranquil as when sunlight hits dew and birds chirp all merry and gay
Fostering an era of unsurmountable symbiosis of hooves and scales.

The hooves took charge of the forest and the hills around the lake
With benevolence which was devoid for epochs innumerable,
As the weak with their littluns rejoiced and venerated the ox;
The amber seemed to be second now to the ivory,
Missing the glory of the erstwhile reign only to finally see green.

And green did the lenses of Poubius turn
With a covetous fury they flung out of the waters to chomp
On the heart of the pal who at one point in the rich history
Of the lake and the forest had saved from death the glow of the amber.
All those loyal to the ivory horns met with the fire effused

From hate that burnt and smoked nests, littluns, and mothers;
The swans from the lake deflowered the daughters of the woods
As the all powerful and witty Zeus looked on unaffected and flippant
As the forest burnt and continues to burn becoming one with the amber.

III. <u>Winner</u>

There can be only one winner,
Most of us are not destined for greatness
As we imagined for ourselves
During our time in college,
Not everyone can be the captain,
Most of us amount to be a part of the crew.

If we weren't born in the right family:
An elite or Brahmin family of judges and writers
With wealth that can only be described as filthy.

We're not heading towards success.
No matter how many motivational videos
You watch, life will remain a struggle.
You ain't gonna become the greatest writer,
You ain't gonna become the greatest singer,
You ain't gonna become the greatest whatever,
All you can do, is be real and accept your fate;
Your place in the realm of the mediocre
And get going sans expectations of greatness.

Just publish that book,
Sing that song,
Or whatever it is that you wanna do,
Not for this wretch of a world we've got to
Put up with, but to respond to the pure urges

ELIZABETH DENNINGS

Of your art.

Most fools never follow my advice and suffer,
So if you wish to ignore, dream along those
Foolish dreams till you are reminded of my haunting verses:
There can be only one winner,
Most of us are not destined for greatness!

IV. <u>Subterfuge</u>

Crucifixions even take place today,
In the halls of education
Which feed on student fears,
By HODs who belittle and gossip,
Inciting one against the other
And vomit vitriol like a screaming banshee
Through the corridors of this college,
But truth, a bitterness,
Must be upheld though our loved ones fall,
Though the administration shows no regard
For the maxim, audi alteram partem,
Where judgments are passed in
Hushed voices and whispers,
Behind your back!

V. *__Two Beasts__*

I. Hanging the Rapist
A beast hangs a fellow beast.
Is there any decipherable difference?
While the bestiality of one is from rage,
That of the other is from circumstance;
We are responsible for our own depravity,
A beast hangs a fellow beast!

II. Israel v/s Iran
Great! A fellow beast fires missiles at another.
When will war become obsolete rather than a solution?
Doesn't this status quo point
Towards the impotency of mankind?
Great! A fellow beast fires missiles at another!

VI. <u>To the Left and Centre</u>

*In this ominous darkness
That seems to be insurmountable
Let us look towards the star,
The Preamble of our Constitution,
Let us bring our palm to the ear to harken
The National Anthem,
And follow the holy light and hymn
To stay forever united in our diversity.*

VII. *Justice and Power*

Justice is nothing
Sans corrupting power;
Power is nothing
Sans unethical wealth.

VIII. <u>Grappling with Injustice</u>

We live in an unjust world,
Although it be unfair to thee,
Let it not stain your poetry.

We live in an unjust world,
Whilst love chose to forgo thy invite
And the cake has turned stale,
Hold not your love for society;
Care as if loved in bounty were thee.

Does it matter to the tree across the pane,
Whether 'twas loved or despised?
Be as firm, stable, and calm.
You may bend and whirl in the storm,
But do not break until this unjust world
Cuts you down!

3. Queer Conundrums

I. <u>Grotesque</u>

No matter how much I accept myself
There will be opposition from society,
I shall continue to be a feminine monster.

I wish I could somehow entrap you
In at least half of the life I've lived,
So that you'd experience how it feels to be
Grotesque!

As a child:
Come dance with me on my footstool
To the F.M music playing on the radio,
The Bollywood hits,
Come feel the girl in me,
Come feel the insolence,
When I was always being me,
Come feel the touch of my landlord,
Come feel the disappointment of my folks,
Come dance with me on my footstool.

As a teenager:

Come feel the mockery by my tuition teacher,
Not once or twice but certainly more than I could take,
Come fight with the woman in me,
Shun her as a witch in the gaol of darkness
Of the galiothic forest,
Of the deepest trenches of the sea,
Come cry with me in silent screams of rage and rejection,
Come feel my aching jaw
As it is incapable to shut till pain
Loosens its grip on the soul,
Come cry with me in silent screams of rage and rejection.

As a young adult:
Come feel the foulness of the bonds I've had,
Where people are ashamed to associate with me,
Come feel the chaos of femininity and masculinity,
Come feel what it truly means to be the other woman; men don't settle with us,
They fall for us and then for society fall for you, woman,
Here, listen to the snigger of the hyenas at the wayside of the masjid,
Come feel the insolence of the rakshasa
Who joins his palms in obeyance of
Ram, Vishnu and Shiva,
And yet say: ye humari sanskruti nahi hai,
Come feel the indifference and insensitivity
Of those who consider themselves pure,

ELIZABETH DENNINGS

For they are one with the church,
Come feel the foulness of the bonds which have seeded distrust
in me.

I wish I could somehow entrap you
In at least half of the life I've lived,
So that you'd experience how it feels to be
Grotesque!

II. <u>Feminine Monster</u>

The sweetness of your face,
The sweetness of your ways,
So sublime,
Like the pleasant morning rays,
Like the footpaths of Panjim city
In the monsoons,
So desolate,
Yet tender.

Why would such sweetness
Wish to be with a lesser man
Like me,
A feminine monster?

How I wish I could have
That flower and its aroma,
How I wish I could
Cherish and protect you,
How I wish you would be mine,
Disremembering the dissonant reality,
That nothing can be owned.

III. <u>Queer and Sassy</u>

I was sensitive and sassy,
I was feminine and racy,
Confident and a woman,
But for society no less than an omen.

The laity told me I was an abomination,
That I'll burn in the fires of hell.

My classmates, teachers and friends
Bullied me to their heart's content.
They asked with contempt,
Why do you walk like that?
Why do you talk like that?

They inflicted gashes on my most tender heart:
Bile, bizuaon huicho, baizon, hijra, ladies;
Their vile snigger still echoes in my mind.

I metamorphosed into a cocoon;
Where I lay dejected for years together.
My only pals: the sea, the stars and the moon,
Until I responded feather by feather.

I took flight releasing myself from the
Shackles of religion, society, and shame.
I walk with the same sassiness,

BY THE RIVER MANDOVI

I talk with the same sassiness
And the world hasn't changed much
For I beget the same contempt
Though subtle,
For they know not to take me on,
For to take me on is to confront
Not just me but my history,
Of struggles, shame, and contempt!
Bring it on!
Bring it on!
BRING IT ON!

IV. <u>Are You a Boy or a Girl?</u>

The sun is at it again,
Making me sweat through my good clothes,
As I sit in the bus waiting for my stop,
And the conductor screams to reveal his vein.

The bus halts with a jerk: ho-ham,
To take on board a woman:
Dusky and dirty,
Clad in a ghagra choli,
Covered with mirrors
That reflect our fears,
And her sunny ghunghat hanging by the bun.

Along-with, she brings a ramble of four littluns:
The youngest - uncovered from the waist down,
The bus lulls and vouchsafes her sex,
Sometimes hidden into the mother's hip.
The second seems clueless
With nostrils crusted with dirt and dry mucus.
The third, a girl enveloped by silence amidst the
Chaos of the passengers paying the fare,
And the eldest seems seven
With ogling eyes filled with questions.

Ahead our wagon moved,
Through the heat and the dust,

BY THE RIVER MANDOVI

Through roads draped in the afternoon desolation.
Ho-ham, ho-ham, ho-ham,
The bus lurched forward and
He hit his forearm against my temple
As he saved himself from a fall.
I winced a bit,
And he had caught a sight of me.
Was I unique to him?

Confused by society and naturally intrigued,
He sweetly enquired,
"Are you a boy or a girl?"
I rubbed my stubble to respond,
He declared as though God,
"No, you are a girl!"
And I smiled to concede
While he waved good bye!

V. <u>An Elegy to Queer Warriors (Fallen from Suicide)</u>

Art emanates from the well of pain,
You draw from it to life sustain,
You hold on to the rough rigid rope,
Till you see the vessel of glinting hope.

And with this you make pure, the world,
Selfless, though lacking within, you let life unfurl.

You draw till the rough rigid slice through skin,
Till the sound of the wheel haunts from within,
And one is drawn towards the brink of the well,
The precipice of no return, an untimely farewell.

And with this you make pure, the world,
Selfless, though lacking within, you let life unfurl.

And one with hope you become;
Not we desire that you leave,
But you depart with a glint of reform,
A spark that makes each one of us believe.

And with this you make pure, the world,
Selfless, though lacking within, you let life unfurl.

VI. <u>Queer Amelioration</u>

I stroll about in the Panjim Art Park,
Among boys and girls I see a spark,
While the latter doesn't see eye to eye,
The former is bold and barely shy.

I bump into these bubbles of yin and yang,
Hoping to one day see queer love hand in hand!

VII. *Repulsive Queerness*

I have truly loved you,
And just as everyone I loved
Never loved me back,
I know your repulsion for me;
I've made peace with this repulsion...

VIII. <u>Nostrils Deep</u>

I wish you would care
More for my heart
For my childlike nature
For the supple radiance when I smile
For my brave femininity
For my reserved silence
For my verses
For my intrigue with thoughts and books.

I wish you would care
Less for my person and
My material possessions.

We are not parted by any great ocean
But merely a shallow pond!
And our love so deep
Has met its demise
Crouched
With its face drowned
Nostrils deep.

I shall not suffer
For I know of man's dullness,
It is you who seeks for the ideal
In which you shall go under, full!

IX. <u>Unabhorred</u>

Pray don't take a harsh tone with me
My most dearest boy.
I don't mind the ugly and their foulness,
But not you, the sweetest joy,
For I endear, cherish and admire thee,
Notwithstanding thy repulsion of me;
The contempt that whole of society,
Unabhorred, relishes in.

I wish to cherish thee for ever,
If thou let me be thy keeper.

X. *To Aditya and Anis*

What makes you think
That you'll find a partner?
I liked you,
May be not loved;
There are men and boys I've loved.

I've always fallen for those
Who're warped, twisted,
Creatures that people largely
Avoid in these times but which
I've always liked or loved!

That's how I know you'll never be chosen.

XI. *Lovely Ugly Lad*

A boy I saw with,
Lips of colour pink,
Like raspberry lollies,
And pure unblemished skin,
Like white butter that Krishna craved,
And an seraphic gaze.

Alas, he spoke and the dream
Degenerated into nothingness.

4. Prejudice

I. *Prism*

Does anyone deserve hate and bloodshed,
For they belong to a group you consider sub-human:
Religion, sexual orientation, sex, gender, race, inter alia?
Do your values fail your character?
Does your culture blind you?
Does your education make you mum?
Do your chants make you deaf?
Do you dream that science
Can be imprisoned in a classroom,
Assigned to a brave Caesar?

They are not human for you,
You flinch to say with crisp clarity,
Fearing judgment of the world,
But you utter the unutterable,
Trying to wield your ugly truth
After gulping down a block of air,
That slashes down your malice ridden throat;
Is that your troth?
Failure to conceive liberty,
Failure to conceive a question,

Failure to be real, raw, and civil.

They are not human for you,
But, how humane are you?
Discrimination is discrimination,
It refuses to be chained to a theme
As per your prejudiced will,
For it is not a woman,
For it is not queer,
For it is not inferior,
It exists in a prism where you belong,
Which is truly your religion and culture,
The prism of discrimination.

II. <u>Limited Value</u>

I knew not that life was priced,
And that one costs more than the other!
What was my price?
Who did fix a tag on me?

I knew not that life was priced,
And that one costs more than the other!
That there were types:
The special and the regular,
The fortunate and the unfortunate.

I knew not that life was priced,
And that one costs more than the other!
That it was fixed at eleven thousand dollars,
For reason of age, class, race, and gender;
A 26 year old woman of limited value!

When did 'regular' become a pejorative?
When did we become so insensitive?
Have we lost all empathy?
For we seem to be okay
With our words and actions that kill humanity!

I knew not that
My life was priced,
By society,

And yet so priceless
For a society closer to my soul, family.

III. <u>God of Nothing</u>

My heart I gave
To those who couldn't keep,
My time I surrendered to them
Never realizing their entitlement.

I tried to find signs of affection,
But all I got were edicts of silence;
They pain, they gnaw at my fragile heart,
For I believed they felt just as I did.

I choose not to be ruled by the heart,
But the body has needs and a mission
Which causes this pain and gnawing
That shall forever be my companion.

I am reminded of a woman of 34,
Who died by suicide,
I scoffed, "How can you be sad at 34?
I've gained happiness in solitude at 30."

I lost track of my godliness,
That I'm respected, not accepted,
That I have authority, not allegiance,
That I am worshiped, not loved.

IV. <u>Not Privy to Our Shame</u>

As I fill the bucket for my bath,
I am visited by immortal shame,
It is a common emotion, a path,
A blight that afflicts without blame.

The water overflows but I digress
From discipline and let it flow;
This, we did not choose on ourselves
And people, not privy to our shame
Choose to sit in judgment under the
Authority of religion and ignorance.

It is our struggle, our book of history,
Do not be despondent, do not despair,
Do not be engulfed in vitriolic fury,
For we were meant to selflessly care.

Stumped I am at the abhorrence of
Those who are not privy to our shame.
What do you have to lose?
Your manhood? your womanhood!
When will you be a better human
And shun satanic verses, 2000 years old?

I turn the tap off and stop the stream to the gutter,
I perform my ablutions and get on with life,

Purifying myself of all religious mutter
Till there is merely human which shall prosper and thrive.

V. *Failure of Society*

I have been hurt by
The indifference of
The ones I loved so
Deeply and truly
That I shut the gate
On anyone who for
A moment moistens
My sight of this world!

I have become today
Indifferent towards
Most that is part of
This wretched realm.
I wished this not on me
But was imperiled by
The indifference;
While I wished to bloom
Like every other flower!

I have just been myself,
I wouldn't know other ways
To live this life to the brim.
Although it may harm me
I shall never know of better
Means to be glee and gay.
It is this society that has

Failed me in every season;
It is this society that has
Failed me in every season.

VI. Come Walk with Me

Come walk with me,
Listen to the birds,
Look at the youngsters fool around,
Titter at the childish love on the
Promenade of the Mandovi,
Read sweet poetry,
Eavesdrop on the gossiping leaves,
Admire the Portuguese era church
Across our mighty river,
All while shying away from the
Merciless Sun.

Come walk with me,
Lest walking with the subaltern
Be beneath your dignity,
Come walk with me,
Come walk with me!

5. Love of a Numdilect

I. <u>Cherish I do thee</u>

Cherish I do thee for thy frailties,
Cherish I do thee for thy manners,
Cherish I do thee for thy innocence.

Love ought to be a wonder,
Not an ugliness that brings my being asunder.

II. <u>Love That Grows with Time - Unrequited</u>

I believed in earnest that I shall
Free myself from the shackles of your sweet thoughts.
I see now that I have failed miserably,
A misendeavour and one among many blots.

My being can never unlove you
My most dear boy;
To love thee is to experience mist and dew,
And to abstain from thee
Is to abjure from poetry.

You are like the valleys of Coorg,
Draped in the fragrance of the flower, coffee:
Jasmine and tea.

You are like crisp Ooty
With its benumbing, comforting and enfeebling cold;
Its serpentine lanes through the village, the town and the lea.

You are like the magnificent sea,
One that can entice and purge,
Consign me to a meaningless debris.

Pray let me live in peace,
If ye wish me not
As I yearn for you,

BY THE RIVER MANDOVI

Like the traveller beaconed
By nature's cologne and bosoms.

I hope I shall tread with caution,
Balance the roles of a guide and a secret lover.
I hope it all falls in place without much destruction
From within and without my soul,
For as long as you are before me
I shall immensely and most deeply endear you.

I hope this shall set easy
Like the moon, the sun and the sea,
As have all others,
Leaving me incomplete and deserted
For an eternity!

III. <u>Choosing Love</u>

If you ever wish to love,
Love someone shaandaar,
Love someone brave enough
To at least love you back beparwah.

IV. <u>A Sweet Cup of Tea</u>

Does love need to be lascivious?
Can't it be holding hands at tea?
Or cuddling up on days: damp, cool and cosy?

I just wish to read to you, my sweetest,
Copious amount of verses;
You'd never want me to stop,
Smitten by my crisp intonations
And my suave pronunciations,
Till we find our theme poem
Which we shall take to our graves.

Can't our love be such greatness
Free from society?
Can't it?

- To my sweetest boy!

V. *__Ensnared__*

It hurts when nightmares conjure into reality:
An entity so beautiful from without
Can be so ugly from within
And in these moments I drown
In a vacuum that benumbs,
While Einaudi relieves my frown,
When my heart flutters and weak it becomes.

VI. *__Dalliance__*

Loneliness hurts;
Someday it'll be a friend,
And you shall fear intrusion
By a worthy soul.

If you wish not,
This dalliance with silence,
Then give yourself a chance
To love someone worthy,
For you deserve the best;
Everyone does!

VII. <u>May Be</u>

If everyone is destined to have a lover,
What do you think happened to mine?
He may live in another country across the mighty river,
Alone and miserable, in his hand a glass of wine.

May be he's no more,
May be he ended up being a whore,
May be I didn't choose him, for I judged him ugly,
Or may be he didn't choose me!

May be he's filthy rich that it separates us
Like a wall of expensive fabrics, perfumes, and châteaux.

VIII. <u>Unending Pursuit</u>

My pursuit of acceptance and love
Looks like an irregular rhyme scheme
Of consonants and vowels
With the rhythm fading into dissonance.

A hymn sang along the ghats,
When will this funeral pyre cease to burn?
Or is it the inextinguishable Atar,
That shall purify and transform eternally the self?

IX. *Delusional Love*

I have yearned for you at the first rays that touch earth,
I have kissed your cheek, your most sublime cheek.

I have yearned for you in the scorching heat of high noon,
I can conquer for you the stars and the moon.

I have yearned for you in the gloom and calm of dusk,
You have been in love with me as the flitting musk.

I have yearned for you in the deep darkness of the nights,
But you are a dream broken at the first rays that touch the heights.

X. *Think of You*

I have loved in earnest,
Through verses, I've weaved
You in my poetry, its rhythms
In agreement to the heart's pulse
Which I can call briefly mine.

And though never chosen,
I shall seek refuge in you,
To soothe my timorous heart,
Just as when debilitating fear
Would strike before bed;
I shall dream a dream of you,
As I move to the unknown life beyond:
Calm and at peace!

XI. *Foolish Orsino*

[If music be the food of love, play on;
Give me excess of it, that, surfeiting,
The appetite may sicken, and so die.]

To engage in excesses,
With music, with spirit,
To defy the lull of the cupid's
Golden tipped arrow,
Is but a folly of a naive lover.

The antidote is not sought after,
For the lull is a soothing pain
For those who have not much to do;
Love is the trade of the bourgeois,
While the proletaire escapes its clutches
Through sheer toil.

The cure lies in a vial with a soiled surface,
A concoction of a three:
A tincture of love that brings suffering,
Two quarters of will and with a heavy heart,
A quarter of dismissal of that infatuation;
Take this and drink it,
Lest you wish to abdicate the throne, your monarchy.

XII. <u>**Duet with Shakespeare: Escaping a Nymph**</u>

[Some swore he was a maid in mans attire,
For in his lookes were all that men desire,
A pleasant smiling cheeke, a speaking eye,
A brow for Love to banquet roiallye;
And such as knew he was a man would say,
"Leander, thou art made for amorous play:
Why art thou not in love, and lov'd of all?
Though thou be faire, yet be not thine own thrall."]

In a lifetime of sorrow and glee we shall witness beauty,
Through crowds and meadows, as we have cake and tea.
Though enamored by those speaking eyes and orient lippes,
But seldom reach the glorious snow-clad Himalayan peak
Which only a few could make brushing by several posts of death.
Fortunate are they who were no longer entranced by your lush lips,
Repulsed to safety by thy ugly sounds and uncultured manners.

XIII. Duet with Marlowe: What If They Reject Your Proposal?

[Come live with mee, and be my love,
And we will all the pleasures prove,
That Vallies, groves, hills and fields,
Woods, or steepie mountaine yeeldes.]

Every being deserves to be cared for,
Alas, a bounty is merely a lore.
And so, if you have any, be grateful;
If you have none, I promise, life ain't dull.

If you have none, you may seek all pleasure
Of vallies, mountaines and fields, with leisure
For liaison and solitude, both have their miracles and crosses,
Though in the latter, all is yours, free from the follies of another.

XIV. <u>Coming Home</u>

I was alone and happy as a child,
Deluded and in love as a man,
And now, reunited with the child again,
I am back to a place my soul considers home.

6. Self-Care

I. *Footpath and Mask*

I traverse on spaces covered in moss,
With an emerald green gloss,
And one slips into a child's snivels,
Into moaning and despairing upheavals,
With the lower lip pushing against the upper,
Covered from public eye by the mask, our keeper,
None to discern our countenance.

And as I traverse these spaces covered in moss,
The only thing you wish for
Is to care of this sweet child,
A child that you saw suffer,
Who trots without a care on the footpath,
Only to be struck with the ways of this world.

As I traverse these spaces covered in moss,
I yearn to protect the child so sublime,
Like the mother it never had,
Like the friend it will never had,
Like a lover as well!

II. <u>Moving On</u>

When one tells you in clear words
That you are not integral to them,
Accept life like the wild by the delicate birds,
And don't hold on to the tattered by the hem.

III. <u>Shliks-Triks-Tarr</u>

In the fragrance of pages, I find my solace,
In those shliks-triks-tarr I find my peace,
As the closing nears, my good friend, I wish to embrace,
Knowing well, I can only have you till the last fading crease.

IV. <u>Empty Pursuit</u>

I was nothing to the ones I loved,
And those who loved meant nothing to me;
At the end of this empty pursuit,
I found it surreptitiously cuddled within.

V. *The Sun Bird II*

I am a sun bird,
And I shall sing my song,
Whether someone loves me or not,
I shall sing my song
In defiance, unabashed,
I shall be a sun bird!

VI. A Book

Those devoid of solace from love and society,
Find it in the flaps of books enveloped in life-dust;
It resides within a fable, tale, myth, a story,
Impressed with eternal ink which makes good the mental rust.

It resides in the hope infusing aroma of the aged pages
Which hold in them a hundred feeling touches,
Some who've departed and some who still reside in cages;
A book is a communion, a vortex of lives.

Inhale its fragrance and hold it against your bosom for relief,
And the mind shall be free of all ailments that invite unbearable grief.

VII. *Toxic Episodes*

Oh, how often the nagging demons
Of the past cause from within, trouble,
Released upon us my malevolent humans;
Yet, hold your focus and be genuine and humble.

Be true to your art: music, teaching, poetry,
For that is all there is to life, let none sully.

VIII. <u>Jam and Butter</u>

During one of my K.G. days,
At recess, I opened my tiffin
To my favourite sandwiches,
    Of jam and butter.

My teacher asked me
With a sadness in her voice,
As though meaning it,
But not really meaning it,
"Nothing for me, Elroy?"

I thought to myself:
I love these sandwiches!
But teacher must be so hungry,
She has none, while I have some.

I sliced one sandwich in my tiny brown hand
    With my tiny brown fingerlings
    As the sweetness drooped out,
    And handed over one piece to
        My teacher.

"Oh, muge bhangracho bhurgo,"
She uttered that chime with so much love,
    It still tinkles at the brush
    Of the childhood breeze.

ELIZABETH DENNINGS

I stood there confounded with
Two pieces of bread slathered with
Jam and butter,
held by my tiny brown fingerlings.
Frankly, I felt berused;
I did not like that trick at all!

I no longer recall her motherly countenance,
We might have met on footpaths and in gardens,
Never to recognize each other,
But I do remember her words:
Oh, muge bhangracho bhurgo,
Oh, muge bhangracho bhurgo!

7. Life Lessons

I. *To Dhanashree*
Life is all about a smile and a cry;
If one only desires a smile,
They're certainly living a lie,
But if one merely wallows in things vile,
How can they truly experience love that is most sublime?

II. <u>Man and Books</u>

I now see no difference
Between people and books,
Some will tear our hearts,
Some will hold us like a hook
And some will inflict both.

Just with people,
We choose our reads;
Shun those which burst our bubble
And embrace those which help us grow.

So read,
When time shows mercy, read!
Man and books.

III. <u>Uncertain Life</u>

Today I stand victorious
Against melancholy,
But how long will it last,
This moment so glorious?

They say that nothing is here to stay,
My defeat is certain,
Or have I already been defeated?
Or will it be eternal victory that I so pray?

IV. *My Little Library*

Everything on Instagram looks so elegant,
With the beautiful shelves and faces so jovial,
Most live in reels and shun the real,
How dare we turn so flippant?

The colossal realities are simple and non-affluent,
Just like yours and mine, the true deal,
My little library with its modesty in every book and quill,
And it is this humility that makes life relevant.

However shallow the virtual may be,
It has revealed a creature from within so malevolent,
It is called a troll who relishes in trampling my library,
Scrolling and hurting as an ignorant.

It is not possible to go back, my lovelies
For the sin to abjure the simple
And embrace the material is a great one!
There is now just a history of posies.

Let us try to conjure the days that were simple,
With a little grit,
A little patience,
And a little of everything good
As I return to the comfort of my little library!

V. <u>Darwin's Finch</u>

I loved to the hilt though all in vain
And wouldn't dare to squander time,
Lest I wish like a fool to surrender again.

But what is life without love's perversions?
To live as a celibate,
Like the banal catholic priest,
With a hope in holy fictions.

Accompanied by peaceful solitude,
Just as the clergy with its urges subdued,
Both of us wage skirmishes by the clinch
Akin to the Darwin's Finch!

VI. *Trust Issues*

When our own folks eschew us,
What can we expect from strangers?
When distrust infuses with rigour
And forms the sinew of our being!

VII. <u>**Shackled**</u>

We all arrive with a cry,
As fluids are shoved with a thrust,
As we get acclimated to the new,
We begin to live!

And all throughout childhood
We're independent and unaffected
From deep within like the celestial bodies:
Mighty, regal, unsurmountable and strong.

We are cultivated to depend on another
Who is alien to our very core;
In enmeshing with this extra-terrestrial,
We become alien to ourselves.

Some figure it out in their adulthood,
Unshackling from religion and materialism,
Some give in to society,
Complacent with appeasement.
While some climb the peaceful mountains,
And others walk by the whispering beaches,
In solitude, independence, like the Sun and the Moon.

And when fluids accumulate yet again,
Some shall be gripped with fear,
While others shall depart with ease.

VIII. <u>The Child Within</u>

I wish to be a child again,
They never yearned for
That which brings immense pain;
I wish to be a child again.

8. Ecology

I. Premonition: An Elegy to a Tree

I was just thinking about you, my lovely tree,
How much you've grown through time,
Inch by inch defying the harshness of nature's whim,
Without a sound, you've endured with glee.

You were there during my childhood,
Jutting out of the precincts of the Colaco Mansion,
Like stretching your arms and psithurous fingertips as far as you could,
You seemed to have crossed a line, a wall.

Today my siesta was broken by the sounds of a hacking,
What was your crime for which you were so punished?
Every slash ripped away from my cosmic person, a childhood rekindling,
Should we let time take over till our sense of guilt stands vanished?

Who was the true criminal and the trespasser?
Who had a greater right, the owner or nature?

II. *Congregation of Sunflowers*

Through the brown fields of nothingness
That I gazed upon while in a moving bus,
There was one with a congregation of sunflowers.

Oh, what a spectacular morning feast:
Like a heavenly abode among hell's fire,
Like a nursery of care amidst world wars,
Like an island hemmed in by a treacherous ocean,
Like hope in a leafling on barren trees,
Like an oasis in the desert,
Like the soothing melody through the earphones
That detaches one from the bustle of the crowd.

Notes To The Poems

1. *Poubius and Mithunaur*: Pengba is a near-threatened fish endemic to eastern Manipur in India, Yunnan and Myanmar.
2. *To the Left and Centre*: Written on the inauguration day of the Ram Mandir at Ayodhya on January 22, 2024.
3. *Queer and Sassy*: The words, *bile*, and *bizuaon huicho* (*baizan khaincho*)/*baizon* (*baizan*) are Konkani words and phrases which are often used in contempt against effeminate men in Goa much like the Hindi word, "*hijra*" when used as a pejorative.
4. *Are You a Boy or a Girl?*: A *ghagra choli* is a traditional outfit worn by women in India, particularly in regions like Rajasthan, Gujarat, and parts of Punjab. A *ghunghat* is a traditional veil or covering worn by women in parts of India, particularly in rural or conservative areas.
5. Numdilect is a word coined from the Latin phrase, *numquam dilectum* which means, "never chosen as a lover."
6. *Jam and Butter*: "*Muge bhangracho bhurgo,*" is a Konkani phrase which translates to, "my golden boy."

Milton Keynes UK
Ingram Content Group UK Ltd.
UKHW030639191124
451300UK00006B/85